HE G

Other books by Ian Barclay

The Facts Of The Matter
He Is Everything To Me (23rd Psalm)
Down With Heaven (The Fruit Of The Spirit)
The "I" Of The Storm (Jonah)
He Stoops To Conquer (Mark's Gospel)

HE GIVES HIS WORD

a look at the Bible

Ian Barclay

HODDER AND STOUGHTON
LONDON   SYDNEY   AUCKLAND   TORONTO

All Bible quotations are taken from the New International Version.

British Library Cataloguing in Publication Data

Barclay, Ian
  He gives his word: a look at the Bible.
  —(Hodder Christian paperbacks)
  1. Bible—Criticism, interpretation,
etc.
  I. Title
  220.6   BS511.2

ISBN 0 340 39079 4

CONTENTS

For Pat and Margaret,
great encouragers in the Word

FOREWORD

My task has been to give as many facts as I can about the Bible within 15,000 words. This has often meant that I have had to write in a Christian shorthand. I have tried to imagine that my readers will be new Christians or a study group who simply want the basic facts about the Bible that are available today.

For the publishers, David Wavre has been a great encouragement. I am also extremely grateful to Dr Derek Tidball and Prebendary Michael Saward for reading the manuscript to make certain I haven't dropped too many theological bricks. Any mistakes or errors of judgement that remain are mine not theirs. I am also grateful to my secretary, Sally Newsham, for her patience in deciphering my handwriting and dictation.

Ruskin said about the Bible, 'It is not only the Book of God, it is also the God of Books.' Chrysostom said, 'The source of all our evils is ignorance of the Word of God.' The Bible is the *sure road* to every blessing. This book will only have been a success if, in the end, we put it down and pick up a Bible.

The Evangelical Alliance
London
1986

Ian Barclay

1

HE GIVES HIS WORD

The Bible continues to be a best-seller around the world. It has been translated into over 280 languages. If you simply want to read a New Testament, it is available in over 590 languages while the gospel and other parts of the Bible have been translated into over 1800 languages and dialects. In 1979 the United Bible Societies distributed over half a billion copies of the Bible around the world and in the same year, world sales ran into thousands of millions. These facts and figures alone should make us want to study this unique book.

More Than A Handbook

Whatever your hobby or interest, there is bound to be a *handbook* to cover its essential principles. There will probably be a *guide book* for beginners and a *study book* for those who want to approach the subject more thoroughly. In one sense the Bible is the handbook of christianity. Sören Kierkegaard, the nineteenth century Danish theologian said, 'the New Testament settles what christianity is.'[1] A hundred years earlier Dr Samuel Johnson said to the faithful James Boswell, 'Sir, ours is a book religion.'[2] He meant that the Bible defines christianity and tells us what God has said. If you want to know about Jesus Christ, or to understand how to live as a christian, or even to see what the Church should be in a particular age, you will not get very far in your studies until you turn to the Bible and see what it has to say.

However, the Bible is not simply a handbook, it claims to be more than a reference book written by men. It appears to have an eternal dimension. When Walter Scott was dying, he said to his secretary, 'Bring me the Book.' The secretary thought about the size of his employer's library with its thousands of leather bound volumes, and hurriedly enquired, 'Which book, Dr Scott?'

'The Book,' insisted Scott, 'the Bible – the only book for a dying man!'[3]

An Extra-Terrestrial Book

In spite of a few intrepid cosmonauts and astronauts, the human race is trapped on planet earth. Man is imprisoned on this tiny globe and surrounded by a seemingly endless universe. Over the last few thousand years he has tried to understand the ultimate force behind everything he can see, and the great religions of the world are the result of this quest. They are man's attempt to find God.

Christianity's approach, is however, entirely different. It is not what man has to say about God, but rather what God has said about man and what, in His love, He has done for him. In the 1970s Francis Schaeffer said of God, 'He is there and He is not silent.' The Bible is God making contact with human beings. It is His communication, coming from outside the confines of the universe. In that sense its contents are extra-terrestrial. Therefore we must surely approach the Bible in a way we wouldn't use for other books. Because the Bible speaks often about God's love for man, it isn't a dry old *reference book*, it is a *love letter* from a personal God to each one of us.

The God Who Speaks

When someone contacts us, we need to know something about them before we can make our response. The God who reveals Himself in the Bible is personal. He is not a cosmic force or a galactic energy field. He is loving, purposeful, and almighty; He is someone who has always been, and always will be there. He knows what is right; He hates what is wrong; He is just; He is merciful. He has created and given life to everything that exists, 'for in Him we live and move and have our being' (Acts 17:28). Through the forgiveness He offers, He gives us a place in His family and a destiny that is, quite literally, out of this world.

What The Bible Contains

The Bible is a whole library. It is a collection of sixty-six separate items originally written in three major languages; Hebrew, Aramaic and Greek. It was written over a period of about one thousand years and contains many different forms of literature. There is history, correspondence and auto-biography; there are sermons, folk-tales, reminiscences, prayers, family trees, dreams and visions, inventories, battle sagas, chronicles, statistics, rules and regulations, poetry, and much more. It is divided into two main sections: the Old and the New Testaments. The second of these is a collection of documents written over a period of fifty years near the beginning of the christian era, while the first was written earlier and over a much longer period. From the earliest times christianity has regarded these two separate collections as one volume. This is emphasised in the singular title 'The Holy Bible'.

Is It Worth Reading?

Before we begin to look at how the Bible was written, we need to ask the question, 'Is it worth reading?' If you consider one tiny part of the Bible, one letter from the New Testament, and see how it has changed the direction of history, the answer must be 'yes'.

Paul's letter to the church in Rome is one of the most influential books of the Bible. It so radically changed the lives of certain men that they were able to change the direction of history.

The Most Influential Christian

In the fourth century, Augustine was a wild young man who was concerned and troubled by his decadent life. As he lay in a friend's garden he heard a voice saying, 'take and read'. He went back to where his friend had been sitting and found a copy of Paul's letter to the Romans. 'I snatched it up, opened it and silently read the passage on which my eyes fell.'[4] It was Romans 13:13–14, 'Let us behave decently, as in the day-time, not in orgies and drunkenness, not in sexual immoral-ity and debauchery, not in dissension and jealousy. Rather, clothe yourselves with the Lord Jesus Christ'. Augustine then commented, 'A light of utter confidence shone in my heart and all darkness of uncertainty vanished.' Dr J. I. Packer says that Augustine 'became the foremost champion of God's free grace and the most influential teacher bar none in Western christian history.'[5]

Eleven hundred years later, a monk and gifted theologian called Martin Luther, also found himself troubled. He was a good monk and certainly wasn't living the lifestyle of the young Augustine, but nonetheless he couldn't find any sense of peace. He found Paul's letter to the Romans baffling until he saw that God's righteousness was His judgement against sin and not the sinner. Then, with a new understanding, Martin Luther wrote of 'that righteousness whereby, through grace and sheer mercy, God justifies us by faith.' Straightaway, he said, 'I felt myself reborn and to have gone through open doors into Paradise.'[6] This experience of Mar-tin Luther's led to the Reformation in Europe.

Two hundred years later, John Wesley, a missionary drop-out, heard Luther's preface to Romans read at a meet-ing in London. He said, 'I felt my heart strangely warmed, I felt I did trust in Christ, Christ alone, for my salvation; and an assurance was given me that He had taken my sins away, even mine; and saved me from the law of sin and death.'[7] The whole of the Methodist movement in the eighteenth century sprang from John Wesley's new understanding of justifica-tion.

Early in this century, Karl Barth published an exposition of Romans that changed the course of 20th century theology. Emeritus Professor F. F. Bruce of Manchester University said recently, 'there is no telling what may happen when people begin to study the epistle to the Romans.'[8] And Romans is only one small part of the Bible! Therefore, to study the whole seriously could well lead to a life-changing experience.

We will now look at the way the Bible came to be written, how to interpret it, and deal with some of the difficulties often encountered.

1. Emil Brunner *Revelation and Reason*, SCM, 1947, p. 44
2. H. D. McDonald *I Want To Know What The Bible Says*, Kingsway, 1979, p. 27
3. John F. MacArthur jnr *Take God's Word For It*, Regal Books, 1980, p. 5
4. David Bentley-Taylor *Augustine, Wayward Genius*, Hodder & Stoughton, 1980, p. 40
5. J. I. Packer *Under God's Word*, Lakeland, 1980, p. 130
6. *Ibid*, p. 131
7. *Journal of John Wesley*, 24 May, 1738, Epworth Press
8. F. F. Bruce *Romans*, Tyndale Press, 1963, p. 60

2

REVELATION

Revelation is fundamental to the christian faith. Christians believe that God has revealed Himself through nature, names, signs and symbols, the prophets, His word and finally through His Son, Jesus Christ. The writer to the Hebrews says, 'In the past God spoke to our forefathers through the prophets at many times and in various ways, but in these last days he has spoken to us by his Son' (Hebrews 1:1). It is surprising therefore that the word *revelation* is quite a rare Bible word. It is not used in the Old Testament and seldom occurs in the New. The word translated *reveal* in the Old Testament means 'nakedness' and so speaks of the way God uncovers His character for us all to see. Our English word, *revelation*, comes from one meaning *to unveil* or *to disclose something that would otherwise have remained hidden.*

The Bits And Pieces Of Revelation

The phrase 'many times and in various ways' (Hebrews 1:1) literally means 'bits and pieces'. There are many important elements of revelation and we have to piece them together to complete the picture. *The names of God* provide an important part of this picture. In Hebrew, a person's name is a perfect reflection of his personality and character. There are at least twenty-two different names for God in the Old Testament, each one disclosing a different aspect of His nature. Among the most familiar are Jehovah-Jireh *'the Lord who provides'* (Genesis 22:14), *'the Lord who heals'* (Exodus 15:26), *'the Lord who is our shepherd*' (Psalm 23:1) and El-Shaddai *'the all sufficient one'* (Genesis 17:1). In the New Testament we have *'Abba, Father'* (Mark 14:36).

There are also many names of Jesus to be considered, with ten in the Old Testament and sixty-four in the New. Each one adds another facet to our knowledge of Him.

The Glory Of The Lord

Just as a human artist divulges so much about himself through his work, so nature tells us about God. John Calvin said, 'on each of His works glory is engraven in characters so bright, so distinct, and so illustrious, that none, however dull and illiterate can plead ignorance as an excuse.'[1] How true John Calvin's statement is. However, Calvin believed in God and therefore saw God's work through spiritual eyes. The great German preacher Helmut Thielicke, said, 'it is not nature that opens the door to God, it's the other way around, God opens the door to nature.'[2] Nature is certainly one of the 'bits and pieces' of revelation, yet we must note that it is only as a believer that King David could have written, 'the heavens declare the glory of God; the skies proclaim the work of his hands' (Psalm 19:1).

Biblical Revelation

Speech is a good means of communication. It is the easiest and clearest way for us to understand ideas. When we hear what people say, we are not often left in any doubt about what they mean. This is because words are the most precise way of expressing our thoughts. Although God speaks through nature, He also explains Himself in words. The Bible is the record of these words. We call what God says through nature *general revelation* but the Bible is part of *special revelation*. Through dreams, visions and sometimes 'face to face' (literally 'mouth to mouth') or in the language of today 'eyeball to eyeball', God spoke to men and He commanded them to record what He had said (Exodus 17:14; Numbers 5:23; Joshua 8:32 and Revelation 11:1, etc). One writer says

that the Bible is God's autobiography.[3] It is His story, told in
the way that He wants it to be understood.

A Walking, Talking, Living Word

The 'bits and pieces' of revelation are like an enormous
jigsaw puzzle. The picture is made up of thousands of
different pieces, all fitting together over a period of several
hundred years. The Old Testament is a fragmentary picture
and leads to the Person who is the complete picture of God.
Jesus is another part of *special revelation*. All that God has
ever wanted to say about Himself is now revealed in Jesus.
He is God's Word; a walking, talking, living Word.

Eyes Down

There is a ceiling painting in Rome by Guido Reni called The
Dawn: it depicts light coming into being and describes
creation. However, because it is high up, it is impossible to
study without getting a pain in the back of your neck so a
mirror has been installed on a table placed below the ceiling.
Now the detail of the picture can be studied at leisure.

One of the reasons why the Bible is so important is that
without it, we have no authentic knowledge of Jesus Christ.
We look down at the Bible as it mirrors Jesus and in a
leisurely way discover the details of the Godhead. 'For in
Christ all the fullness of the Deity lives in bodily form'
(Colossians 2:9).

Then Why Can't Some People See?

With all the fragments of revelation adding up to a fairly
complete picture, and finally God speaking to us through His
Son (Hebrews 1:1), we must ask the question, 'Why are some
people still unable to see the truth?' The answer the Bible
gives is that 'The man without the Spirit does not accept the
things that come from the Spirit of God, for they are foolish-
ness to him and he cannot understand them' (1 Corinthians
2:14). The reason why the natural man is in this condition is

because the Evil One, 'The god of this world has blinded the minds of them that believe not' (2 Corinthians 4:4). Just as a deaf man cannot hear music, so those outside Christ do not have the spiritual equipment necessary to hear God. Martin Luther expresses this so well: 'Man is like Lot's wife – a pillar of salt. He is like a log or a stone. He is like a lifeless statue that has neither eyes nor mouth; neither senses nor heart, unless he is enlightened, converted and made regenerate by the Holy Spirit.'[4] Outside Christ, men and women cannot see the Truth.

Can We Add To God's Truth?

We must be very careful not to add to revealed truth because one of the marks of a cult, that is a group of people who are not truly christian, is that they have the Bible and another volume which they say interprets the Bible. THE MORMONS have three books they regard as being equal with the Bible: *Doctrine and Covenant*; *Pearl of Great Price* and the *Book of Mormon*.[5] CHRISTIAN SCIENTISTS hold that Mary Baker Eddy's *Science and Health With Key To The Scripture* is equal with biblical truth. They call Mary Baker Eddy 'the revelator of truth for this age'.[6] JEHOVAH'S WITNESSES regard their publication *The Watchtower* as being without a rival 'because God is the Author'.[7] Over the last twenty-five years we have seen the rise of the CHILDREN OF GOD. Their leader, David Berg, has written over 500 letters to his followers. Berg called himself 'Moses', and although he has lived an extremely promiscuous life, he has said his letters are '*God's word for today*'.[8]

God Speaks Today?

Many would affirm and insist that God still speaks today. However, He most frequently chooses the Bible as His vehicle of revelation. The Bible is still a living book, and where it is faithfully preached and taught, men and women continue to come into a life-changing experience of God.

1. John Calvin *The Institutes of Christian Religion*, James Clarke, 1949, p. 51
2. Helmut Thielicke *How The World Began*, James Clarke, 1964, p. 49
3. Bernard Ramm *Special Revelation and The Word of God*, Eerdmans, 1961, p. 19
4. John F. MacArthur jnr *Take God's Word For It*, Regal Books, 1980, p. 27
5. Alma 5:45, 46 *The Book of Mormon*, The Church of Jesus Christ and Latter-Day Saints, 1950, p. 208
6. *The Christian Science Journal* Vol. 3, No. 7, July 1975, p. 361
7. *The Watchtower*, 15 April 1943, Watchtower and Bible Tract Society of Pennsylvania, p. 127
8. *Christianity Today* Vol. 21, No. 10, 18 February 1977, Christianity Today Inc. of Illinois, p. 18

3

INSPIRATION

Revelation and inspiration are not the same. Revelation is God speaking, and inspiration is the process by which what He says is recorded for us by human writers.

It Is Simpler To Say What It Isn't!

First, it is not the achievement of a few rather special people. It is easy to say that when Handel wrote the score of *Messiah* or when Shakespeare wrote *Romeo and Juliet*, they were inspired. An actor may give an inspiring performance, or a television cameraman might be inspired as he films a piece of drama which leaves the audience quite breathtaken. This is not what we mean when we talk about the inspiration of the Bible. The Bible is not an outstanding human production or the brilliant result of human genius.

Secondly, it is not God working through the minds of men and women as they write. God didn't give an idea to the writer who then sat down and created his own piece of literature on God's original germ of thought. When the Bible speaks about inspiration there is an emphasis on the words rather than the ideas. Paul says to the Corinthians, 'This is what we speak, not in *words* taught us by human wisdom, but in *words* taught by the Spirit, expressing spiritual truths in spiritual *words*' (1 Corinthians 2:13). Jesus said, 'I gave them the words you gave me and they accepted them' (John 17:8). Nearly 4,000 times in the Old Testament we have the phrase, 'thus says the Lord' or 'the Word of God'. It is very difficult to have a wordless idea. When

God inspired the writers of the Bible, He gave them words.

Thirdly, inspiration is not simply God working in our minds as we read the Bible. There can be no truth in the suggestion that the Bible is only the words of men, words which God can take up and use if we read them in the right frame of mind. However, reading the Bible is not a dull affair because 'the word of God is living and active. Sharper than any double-edged sword' (Hebrews 4:12). God can, and often does, make it come alive in an astounding way. The Bible is God's word, and as Jerome, the fourth century teacher put it, 'Not knowing the Bible means not knowing Christ'. Dr E. V. Rieu translated Homer's *Iliad*, and then the Gospels, into Modern English. He spoke about the difference between classical Greek and the New Testament. He explained how the New Testament is 'extraordinarily alive' and how it 'changed him'.[1] The Bible can come alive as we read it but that is not what is meant by biblical inspiration.

Fourthly, the Bible was not written as a result of mechanical dictation. God didn't put a spiritual floppy disk into the men He wanted to be His writers who then produced a mechanical print-out of what He wanted them to say. They weren't spiritual word processors totally unaware of what they were producing.

A Most Ingenious Paradox

The only satisfactory way to approach the whole question of inspiration and the authorship of the Bible is to see a duality of authorship and to say that the Bible is one hundred per cent divine and one hundred per cent human. The word the theologians use for this paradox is *antinomy*. So many christian truths are held in tension between two seemingly irreconcilable ideas. For example, we know that God is absolutely sovereign yet He gives man perfect free will. We can be so certain the Bible is God's word that it might have come through a dictating machine, but it didn't. Equally, it is so human and the frailties and idiosyncrasies of each writer so obvious, they could have blocked what God wanted to say, but they didn't.

What It Is

Inspiration is the direct influence of God on each writer, and while they never cease to be themselves, God says exactly what He wanted to say through them.

The Human Instruments

In chapter one, we noticed that many literary forms are found in the Bible. Once you turn to the question of authorship, you find the human writers came from a great variety of backgrounds. There were kings, priests, fishermen, prophets, prisoners, shepherds, theologians, soldiers, clerks, mystics, lovers, secretaries, judges, lawyers, tyrants and song writers. There was a tax collector, a prime minister, a doctor and a butler. The list is almost endless. Some of the writers had formal education while others didn't. The vocabulary, style, expression and literary devices carry the stamp of each individual. A passage by Isaiah cannot be confused with the writings of Paul. Amos was a shepherd in his day, just as Luke was a doctor in his. Each of the forty writers remains identifiably individual.

How Did It Happen?

Paul gives us the biggest clue when he says that 'all scripture is God-breathed' (2 Tim 3:16). It couldn't be clearer than that. The Bible came from God's mouth. It is His word. In the 1970s Bernard Miles the actor, now Lord Miles, translated some of the Gospel stories into the language of the Chiltern Hills. For him they became 'the story of Jesus doing the job His old dad sent Him to do'[2] and for Bernard Miles the Bible became 'God's Brainwave'. This is exactly what it is. It is God's idea. Dr J. I. Packer says that men no more gave us the Bible than Sir Isaac Newton gave us the law of gravity.[3] God gave us gravity by His work of creation. In the same way a man could discover God's law of gravity, other men were able to discover God's revelation of biblical truth. Peter tells us how this happened: 'Men spoke from God as they were carried along by the Holy Spirit' (2 Peter 1:21). As the tide can carry a boat along, so men were carried by the Holy Spirit in the direction that He wanted them to follow. In this way the Scriptures came to be written.

From Him Through Them To Us

The writers of the Bible, both in the Old and New Testaments, were men who felt under orders from God to pass on what had been revealed. 'The Word of the Lord came to me, saying, "before I formed you in the womb, I knew you, before you were born I set you apart; I appointed you as a prophet to the nations"' (Jeremiah 1:4,5). Once we move to the New Testament, we find the apostle John touched by God in a similar way. 'On the Lord's day I was in the Spirit, and I heard behind me a loud voice like a trumpet, which said, "Write on a scroll what you see and send it to the seven churches"' (Revelation 1:10,11).

How Much Of The Bible Is Inspired?

Paul says clearly that 'all scripture is God-breathed' (2 Timothy 3:16). 'All scripture' could be translated 'every writing' or 'every piece of sacred writing'. When Paul made that statement, all he had in mind was the Old Testament. However, sometime after Paul lived, the christian church included the New Testament documents within the *canon* of scripture. I will deal with the *canon* in a later chapter. For the moment all that needs to be said is that the phrase 'all scripture' is normally taken to mean the whole Bible, both the Old and the New Testaments. Christians regard the complete Bible as God-inspired, and able to speak to men and women in a relevant way today.

1. E. M. Blaiklock *Layman's Answer*, Hodder & Stoughton, 1968, p. 44
2. Bernard Miles *God's Brainwave*, Hodder & Stoughton, 1968, subtitle
3. J. I. Packer *God Has Spoken*, Hodder & Stoughton, 1965, p. 81

4

AUTHORITY

Wherever you care to look today authority is being questioned. In society as a whole, at school and university, in the management structures at work, or even in the home, you will see the breakdown of the old, established patterns of order and control.

What happens in the world is often reflected in the church, and today so many of the problems in the older denominations seem to spring from a questioning of authority. There is either too much or too little direction from above. Where there is firm management it is undermined by the spirit of anarchy which pervades our age as a whole.

One reason often given for the striking growth of the new Restoration Churches (or House Churches) is that some people find these churches provide the firmer framework of authority they want. The danger is that we find our authority in men and not the Bible.

The Fundamental Issue

When we come to the question of authority in the church we come to the most fundamental issue. For if there is no final authority, no absolute norm, no sure word of direction, no moral certainty, then we can all do what is right in our own eyes and nobody can say we are wrong.

The Instrument Of Government

The Bible is God's sceptre,[1] His instrument of government. In the fourth century Augustine, the Bishop of Hippo, said,

'When the Bible speaks, God speaks'.[2] We cannot prove God's authority, of course, but we can recognise it. In spite of man's constant rejection of authority in our own day, the majority of people would appear to have an in-built desire to be managed, directed or even ruled by an authority higher than themselves.

The Basis Of Authority

Dr Martyn Lloyd-Jones affirmed, 'The most important argument of all is that we should believe in the authority of the scriptures because the scriptures *themselves* claim that authority'.[3] Just as black and white declare their colour, and bitter and sweet demonstrate their taste, so the Bible bears evidence of its own authority. It is difficult to dodge the claims of the Bible. The church of God must live under the authority of the Word of God. Many years ago Professor Robertson Smith said before the General Assembly of the Free Church of Scotland:

> If I am asked why I receive the Scripture as the word of God, and the only rule of faith and life, I answer with all the fathers of the ancient church, because it is the only record of the redeeming love of God, because in the Bible alone, I find God drawing near to man in Christ Jesus and declaring to us His will for salvation. And this record I know to be true by the witness of His Holy Spirit in my heart, whereby I am assured that none other than God Himself is able to speak such words to my soul.[4]

These are such commendable words it is sad the professor moved away from them towards the end of his life.

No Man Ever Spoke Like This Man

Jesus is the final and full revelation of God; He is the summary of all that God wants to say about Himself. As soon as Jesus started to teach, people were 'amazed' by His teaching (Matthew 7:28). When He began to work miracles, people 'were filled with awe; and they praised God who had given such authority to men' (Matthew 9:8). The authority of Jesus is unique. No one else would have dared to say 'I and the Father are one' (John 10:30). Jesus did not hesitate to assert His divine authority and even took one of the great Hebrew names of God for Himself. He called Himself 'I am' (Exodus 3:14; John 6:35; John 8:12; John 8:58; John 10:7; John 10:14; John 11:25; John 14:6). Jesus didn't repudiate the Bible, rather He gave it His stamp of approval. The simple phrase 'it stands written' was enough for Him (Matthew 4:10, a literal translation).

The Bible Is Christ's Textbook

Jesus is the head of the church which He rules by His word. In the gospels He instructs His people in matters of belief and behaviour. He doesn't leave anyone in any doubt about how they should live and serve God during their time on earth. It is impossible, as a christian, to read the New Testament and fail to feel the authority of Jesus Christ.

Captive To The Word

Let me conclude this section with an illustration of how the Bible can radically change men if they allow its authority to make them captive to God's word. This story has just been used as the plot of a new musical in the West End of London called 'Mutiny' which stars David Essex and Frank Finlay. The original story tells of what happened when the Bible was wholeheartedly received by a small group of men.

HMS Bounty, under the command of Captain Bligh, left England in 1787, bound for the South Seas to collect bread-fruit trees. They landed at Tahiti in the Pacific and the crew spent the first few weeks enjoying the warm sea in the company of the Tahitian girls, who were attractive and showered their favours freely upon the men. Many of the sailors wanted to settle permanently on the island. Captain Bligh managed to call them back to their duties and with a few grumbles they loaded the ship's cargo and set sail once more. On 28 April 1789, only a few days out from Tahiti, the crew mutinied and Captain Bligh, together with eighteen loyal sailors, were set adrift in an open boat. They eventually reached Timor in the East Indies, some 4,000 miles away. This was a miracle in itself.

Meanwhile, the mutineers returned to Tahiti, persuaded twelve girls to accompany them aboard the Bounty, and set sail with the sole plan of avoiding capture. They landed at Pitcairn Island, an extinct volcano with steep cliffs and very different from Tahiti's broad expanses of sand. Pitcairn was uninhabited and had luscious vegetation, so the mutineers decided to make it their home. They took their own possessions ashore with supplies from the Bounty, and then set the ship on fire. Now no one could prove they were the Bounty mutineers and they were free to establish the sort of life they had enjoyed on Tahiti.

What they thought would be a heaven on earth proved to be a nightmarish hell which lasted ten years. One of the men had taken the ship's copper kettle ashore and it was used to make spirits by distilling plant roots. The whole island was drunk for weeks on end. Some of the sailors went out of their minds, one committed suicide by jumping off a cliff, and all of them lived in a bestial way.

After several years only two men were left, Alexander Smith and Edward Young. Young, by far the older, was ill with asthma. Both men had been forced to live apart from the women who, by capturing the men's firearms, had moved to another part of the island with the eighteen children. The men were threatened with death if they followed.

Edward Young knew that he was dying and in despair searched through his belongings to see if he could find anything that would remind him of the peace and serenity of his early life in England. In the ship's chest he found the Bible and began to read. Alexander Smith could not read, so Edward Young decided to teach him by beginning at Genesis and going through each chapter, word by word. By the time they reached Leviticus they were aware of their own need and had begun to pray. Before they reached the New Testa-

ment, Edward Young had died; but not before Smith had
learned to read. For Alexander Smith, reading the New
Testament meant the full discovery of peace, forgiveness and
restoration.

Even at a distance the children had noticed the change in
the living habits of the men, and soon the women and
children returned to see what had happened. In 1808, nine-
teen years after the mutiny on the Bounty, a ship from Boston
discovered the community on Pitcairn Island. When the
captain of the ship returned to America he took news of the
only surviving mutineer and of what he called: 'The most
perfect christian society that he had ever seen.'

The Bible makes it plain that the true source of all
authority is God, and that divine authority is exercised
through Jesus Christ. Men say with Rousseau, 'Whatever I
feel is right is right. Whatever I feel is wrong is wrong.'
However, it doesn't actually work like that. When we put
ourselves under God's authority, it doesn't matter if we live
on Pitcairn Island or in a London high-rise flat, we create one
of the conditions necessary for a just society and the King-
dom of Heaven.

1. J. I. Packer *Under God's Word*, Lakeland, 1980, p. 41
2. H. D. McDonald *I Want To Know What The Bible Says*, Kingsway,
   1979, p. 34
3. D. Martyn Lloyd-Jones *Authority*, IVF, 1958, p. 50
4. John Eddison *The Bible*, SU, 1984, p. 14

5

INERRANCY

We come now to the vexed question of *inerrancy*. In general terms it would seem safe to say that the church accepted the Bible as 'God's word written' for at least the first 1300 years of the christian era.

During the fourteenth and fifteenth centuries, under the leadership of John Wycliffe, John Huss and Erasmus, we find a growing desire to reform the church on biblical lines. This led to the Bible itself being thoroughly examined and scrutinised. The authorship and the value of some books were now questioned. Martin Luther criticised *James* as being a 'right strawy epistle',[1] while John Calvin doubted the authorship of *2 Peter, James* and *Jude* and omitted *Revelation* from his commentary.[2]

Inerrancy A Modern Phrase

However, it wasn't until the latter part of the last century that the word *inerrancy* was first heard in the English language. Initially, it was used by North American Roman Catholics as a straightforward transliteration of the Latin word *inerrantia*.[3] They were quickly followed by Presbyterians who also started to use it in their statements about the Bible. In 1894, A. J. Gordon referred to the inerrancy of Scripture as a 'modern phrase'.[4]

But A Very Old Idea

That may well be true but the idea of inerrancy can be traced back through the English evangelical leaders of the last century in men like C. H. Spurgeon, J. C. Ryle, H. C. C. Moule, through those of the eighteenth century, and ultimately back through the Reformers to Augustine. For example, on Wednesday 24 July 1776, John Wesley wrote in his *Journal*, 'if there be any mistake in the Bible, there may well be a thousand. If there be one falsehood in that book, it did not come from a God of truth'.[5]

The Present Debate

The present debate began in the United States of America in the 1960s. While it hasn't touched English christians as it has Americans, we would be unwise to underestimate the fierceness of the struggle known in America as *the battle for the Bible*.

Is This Subject Important?

It is very easy to wish that subjects like *inerrancy* could be left to the theologians to debate while the rest of the church gets on with serving and worshipping God in the ordinary everyday world.

Let me emphasise that *inerrancy* is extremely important because the majority of people who have ever drifted away from traditional christian belief began by moving away from the place where they regarded the Scriptures as 'God-breathed', inerrant and therefore important. This initial step may not be recognised, but it is not difficult to correlate a movement that starts with a low view of the Bible and ends with rejecting orthodox christianity. This happened in the last century. The German theologian, D. F. Strauss from Tübingen, in his *Leben Jesu* (1835) sets out to prove that the gospels were a collection of myths and that the original stories were free from any trace of the supernatural. By 1872 he is endeavouring to prove that christianity is dead and that a new faith must now be built out of Art and Science.[6]

Most of the established denominations in this country have recently witnessed men, in senior positions, who have repudiated doctrine which is at the very heart of orthodox christianity. Again, in most cases this can be traced back to a low view of Scripture.

Infallibility

Once we admit that the Bible is '*God breathed*' and stamped with God's character, we will want to say with the men who wrote the Westminster Catechism in 1647, that the Bible is 'infallible truth'.

Inspiration and *infallibility* are two sides of the same coin. And infallibility and inerrancy are closely related. Infallibility speaks about truth while *inerrancy is dealing with facts*.

How Inerrant Is The Bible?

In 1974 christians from around the world gathered for the International Congress on World Evangelisation, in Lausanne, Switzerland. The delegates agreed and drafted the Lausanne Covenant. In this document, the truthfulness of the Bible is emphasised and a statement made that it is '*without error in all that it affirms*'. John Stott, in his explanation of the Lausanne Covenant, goes on to say:

> Since Scripture is God's Word written, it is inevitably true. For, 'God is not man that He should lie' (Num. 23:19). On the contrary, as Jesus Himself said in prayer to the Father, 'Thy Word is truth' (John 17:17). And since it is true, it is '*without error in all that it affirms*'. Notice the careful qualification. For not everything contained in Scripture is affirmed by Scripture. To take an extreme example, Psalm 14:1 contains the statement, 'there is no God.' This statement is false. But Scripture is not affirming it. What Scripture affirms in that verse is not atheism, but the folly of atheism, 'The fool says in his heart, "There is no God."' It is important, therefore, in all our Bible study to consider the intention of the author, and what is being asserted. It is this, whatever the subject of the assertion may be, which is true and inerrant.[7]

Here is a defined area of agreement found by 2,700 leading christians from the major denominations of 150 countries around the world. *Time* magazine said that the Congress was a 'formidable forum, possibly the widest-ranging meeting of christians ever held.' We have seen that among other substantial concerns the Congress said, '*The Bible is without error in all that it affirms.*'

Now, if we don't accept that, we are really rejecting biblical revelation, inspiration and authority at the same time. This will mean that instead of turning to God's Word for help, we will be turning to the latest theologically liberal Guru to see which part of the Bible he believes is true enough for us to read. In exasperation, we will exclaim with Joseph Parker, 'Have we to wait for a communication from Tübingen or a telegram from Oxford before we can read the Bible?'[8] No, let us read the Bible as God's Word, unequivocally certain that '*it is without error in all that it affirms.*'

1. R. E. O. White *Interpreting The Bible Today*, Pickering & Inglis, 1982, p. 110
2. *Ibid*, p. 111
3. J. I. Packer *Under God's Word*, Lakeland, 1982, p. 45
4. A. J. Gordon *The Ministry Of The Spirit*, Kingsgate Press, 1894, p. 182
5. H. D. McDonald *I Want To Know What The Bible Says*, Kingsway, 1979, p. 75
6. *Chambers Biographical Dictionary*, W. & R. Chambers, 1961, p. 1228
7. J. R. W. Stott *Explaining the Lausanne Covenant*, Scripture Union, 1975, p. 7
8. Joseph Parker *None Like This*, Nisbet, 1893, p. 73

6

INTERPRETING THE BIBLE

The two disciples on the road to Emmaus were discussing the events of the first Easter, when Jesus joined them, 'And beginning with Moses and all the prophets, He *explained* to them what was said in all the Scriptures concerning Himself' (Luke 24:27). The word *explained* has given us *Hermeneutics* which is the technical name for the science of interpreting the Bible. There are fairly straightforward principles to guide us in our understanding of the Bible. If these are followed we will be prevented from giving an obscure verse a meaning which it cannot possibly have.

The Illuminating Holy Spirit

When Jesus asked Peter 'Who do you say I am?' Peter replied 'you are the Christ, the Son of the Living God.' Straightaway Jesus commented 'flesh and blood has not revealed this to you' (Matthews 16:17 RSV). We won't get far in our desire to understand the Bible until we recognise the illuminating work of the Holy Spirit. Martin Luther said 'No man sees an iota of the Scripture until he has the Spirit of God.'[1] We must continually pray for guidance as we seek to understand what the Bible is saying.

A Spirit Of Humility

We also need a spirit of humility. Charles Simeon was an Anglican vicar in Cambridge in the nineteenth century. He was a scholarly man and a gifted preacher, yet he came to the Bible in a most humble and childlike way,

In the beginning of my enquiries I said to myself, I am a
fool; of that I am quite certain. One thing I know assured-
ly, that in religion, of myself, I know nothing. I do not
therefore sit down to the perusal of Scripture in order to
impose a sense on the inspired writers; but to receive one,
as they give it me. I pretend not to teach them, I wish like a
child to be taught by them.[2]

The First Rule Of Interpretation

Look at the text HISTORICALLY. We must look at the text and ask
the question 'What did it mean originally?' Six hundred
years ago John Wycliffe, 'the morning star of the Reformation', sent preachers out all over England to take the Word of
God to each city, town and village. Wycliffe's preachers were
hardly men trained for the ministry and yet John Wycliffe's
advice to them cannot really be bettered today. He said, 'It
shall greatly help ye to understande scripture if thou marke
not only what is writ or spoken, but of whom, and to whom,
with what words, at what time, where, and to what intent,
with what circumstances, considering what goeth before,
and what followeth.'[3] The questions basic to our understanding of the text cannot be put more plainly than that.

Lord Eccles, in his autobiography *Half Way to Faith*, tells of
a church which had been built in a once prosperous sheep
farming area. Over the years the farming had changed and
wool was no longer produced. Consequently the population
had moved away to look for work and the few people who
remained found the upkeep of the church rather difficult and
expensive. Major repairs were necessary but funds were not
available. When villagers realised they had a twelfth century
crucifix, they sent it to London to be valued, hoping it would
raise the necessary capital sum. The crucifix had been
important in the life of the village and every year it was given
a new coat of paint in preparation for Easter. The art
historian in London began to remove the layers of paint from
one of the hands and was quite amazed at the life and vitality
of the original carving.

We have to do something similar as we come to understand the Bible. We have to peel away the layers of understanding imposed over the years and get back to the original meaning.

The Second Rule Of Interpretation

Look at the text and see its GENERAL MEANING. To do this, we take our understanding of a text and place it back into the context of the sixty-six biblical documents and ask the question 'is this the general teaching of the Bible?' If what we see in a passage is contradicted by other sections of Scripture then we may be fairly certain that our understanding is incorrect. There is a unity of thought in the Bible that safeguards against unusual interpretation of an isolated verse.

The Third Rule

Look at the text PRACTICALLY. We must ask the question 'What is this now saying to me and what is it asking me to do?' To read the Bible as a christian brings us into the presence of God. Erasmus, in his introduction to the New Testament in 1516, said that it would 'Give Christ to you in an intimacy so close that He would be less visible to you if He stood before your eyes.'[4] The Bible is the Word of God in both the sense that it is a record of what He has said and also in that through it, He still speaks today. No interpretation will be complete until we have personally responded to its demands.

Is Academic Understanding Essential?

For twentieth century disciples, a clear understanding of the Bible will help in every part of christian living. However, God's Word is surprisingly powerful and He is so generous that He often allows the most unexpected man to serve Him with honour. For example, a preacher's commitment and sincerity are often more important than his intellectual equipment. As Dr Alan Cole of Sydney has said, 'God sometimes blesses a poor exegesis of a bad translation of a

doubtful meaning of an obscure verse of a minor prophet.'[5]
However, the fact that God chooses to bless such a ministry
must never be made an excuse for careless interpretation.

Prejudices In Interpretation

It is very easy to make our interpretation fit our prejudices
rather than the other way around. We need to be so aware of
this problem that we avoid its dangers. In general terms
there are three major areas of prejudice that often hinder a
biblical understanding. First, there is the *over-supernatural
approach* which tends to see the miraculous in the most
mundane texts. Then, the *over-natural approach* which looks at
every passage with such a cynical eye that it never sees the
supernatural even when it is obvious. Finally, there is the
over-dogmatic approach which brings Charismatic, Reformed or
denominational theology into a text when it is not there. An
example of this might be Anglicans distorting the meaning of
a text in order to see infant baptism in the Old Testament, or
Baptists to see believers' baptism. Prejudice of any sort is a
dangerous preconception in interpreting the Bible. The Bible must give us our theological mould and it must not be our
preconceived theological mould, Reformed, Charismatic or
otherwise, which gives us our biblical interpretation.

How Long Will It Take To Study The Bible?

How many years' study will it take to give us a reasonable
understanding of the Bible? Martin Luther's last scribbled
note asserts that, as no one can understand Virgil who has
not been a shepherd or a farmer for five years, and no one can
understand Cicero who has not been a politician for twenty
years, so 'Nobody can understand the Scriptures who has not
looked after a congregation for a hundred years.'[6] Surely,
Martin Luther is making the point that it is going to take a
lifetime of study before we have a deep and true understanding of the Scriptures. That shouldn't depress us. What he is
trying to do is to get us into our Bibles *now*. So that straightaway we begin the process of getting to know God's word.

1. R. E. O. White *Interpreting the Bible Today*, Pickering & Inglis, 1982, p. 14
2. J. J. Gurney *Memoirs of the Life of the Reverend Charles Simeon*, Hatchard, 1847, p. 674
3. R. E. O. White *Interpreting the Bible Today*, Pickering & Inglis, 1982, p. 32
4. James A. Stewart *Heaven's Throne Gift*, CLC, 1971, p. 153
5. J. R. W. Stott *Understanding the Bible*, Scripture Union, 1972, p. 206
6. R. E. O. White *Interpreting the Bible Today*, Pickering & Inglis, 1982, p. 12

7

HOW WE GOT OUR BIBLE

Our word *Bible* comes from the Greek word *biblia* which means *books*. Originally it referred to the books of the Law, the Prophets and other writings of the Old Testament. Today when we refer to the Bible we mean the whole volume of sixty-six books. The word *books* can be misleading because initially most were *rolls of papyrus* which were made from the inner bark of a marsh reed. The *byblo* was dried in flat strips and joined together to form a long sheet of writing material which was then rolled up into a *scroll*. These were replaced in the second century AD by the *codex* which was folded paper fastened together at the spine. This was really an early version of today's book. Christians probably pioneered the book as we know it because it wasn't until the fourth century that books passed into general use, by which time they had developed considerably.

Another word for the Bible was *graphia* or *writings* (2 Timothy 3:16). This was translated into Latin as *scripturae* and is obviously the root of the English word *Scripture*. A further description we use is the *Word of God*, which is not strictly a biblical description but nonetheless it is a good choice of words to describe the writings that are 'God-breathed' and come from the mouth of God.

The Earliest Versions

The Old Testament was written in Hebrew and a little Aramaic, but a Greek translation was commissioned in the third century BC for Greek-speaking Jews. It is thought that the translation work was done by seventy-two scholars and is therefore always known as the *Septuagint* or the *LXX*.

The New Testament was originally written in Greek, but it was a Greek that scholars couldn't categorise for hundreds of years because it was neither classical nor modern.[1] However, towards the end of the last century, archaeologists discovered a vast quantity of papyrus in the dry sands of Egypt which was really a rubbish dump and had come from the wastepaper baskets of the local records office. The Greek in these documents was the ordinary language of everyday and matched the Greek of the New Testament.

The Vulgate

The first European language into which the Greek Bible was translated was *Latin*, one of the main languages of the Roman Empire. This translation was made towards the end of the fourth century by Jerome. It is always known as the *Vulgate* because it was intended for the ordinary people in the West of the Empire who had Latin as their *vulgar tongue*.

The Bible For English People

Most people who lived in England before the fourteenth century regarded the Bible as a closed book. The majority of people couldn't read. Even those who did couldn't understand Latin which was the language used by the church and was the language of the Bible too. Aldhelm (circa AD 700), a bishop of Sherborne, translated the Psalms into English and Bede (AD 673–735) translated a little of the New Testament, but no more than that was available.

In about 1360, John Wycliffe became the Master of Balliol College, Oxford, and with the help of friends and colleagues he produced the first complete English version of the Bible. William Tyndale, influenced by the new learning, set to work on a new translation to make the Scriptures available and understandable to every ploughboy in the land. He should have been helped by the invention of printing but the church opposed him and he had to escape to the Continent. However, by 1526 his translation had begun to circulate in England. A few years later, in 1537, Miles Coverdale printed his version of the Bible on the Continent and dedicated it to Henry VIII. The King satisfied himself that it contained no heresies and pronounced 'In God's name let it go abroad among the people.' Many phrases from Coverdale's Bible have been kept in subsequent translations and it is his version of the Psalms which appears in the Anglican Prayer Book of 1662.

The Authorised Version

James I came to the throne in 1603 and expressed his unhappiness over the English translations which had been made. He set forty-seven biblical scholars working to produce a new translation to be submitted to the Privy Council. We call this the *Authorised Version*. Americans seem to find that title misleading because it was never officially approved by Parliament, only by the King. They prefer to call it the *King James Version*.

Chapter And Verse

Pagnini's translation of the Vulgate, printed by Du Ry at Lyon in 1528, was the first to use verse numbering for easy reference. The divisions in the text were made with heavy paragraph marks and the verse number appeared in the margin alongside each mark. However, Pagnini's numbering is not used today because, over the next few years, there was a good deal of experimenting with different numbering systems. Consistency emerged with the Geneva Bible which appeared in English in 1560. There has been little change in chapter and verse numbering since then.

The Canon

We need to take a step back in history to look at the subject of the *Canon* of Scripture. In Greek *Kanōn* originally meant a *reed*. In Bible times it was a Hebrew unit of measurement which came to mean a *measuring rod*. Today it is used to describe the list of works attributed to an author. Therefore, when we refer to the *Canon of Scripture* we are referring to the sixty-six books of the Bible.

How The Choice Was Made

It is important to note that although the acceptance of the Canon was complicated from a human point of view, the sixty-six books are not 'God-breathed' because a group of men said they were. The church was ratifying documents that intrinsically declared themselves to be God's Word.

The Old Testament And Apocrypha

The last book of the Old Testament, Malachi, was written in about 425 BC. Hebrew tradition holds that the final compilers of the *Old Testament canon* were part of the Great Synagogue, the School of Scribes founded by Ezra after the return from captivity in Babylon. Since the close of the Old Testament canon, there has been an attempt to add the writings that we call the *Apocrypha*. Most Protestant christians do not accept them as part of the Bible but Roman Catholics do.

The New Testament Canon

There was a series of questions used by the early church to test the authenticity of the New Testament documents. First, 'Was the author an Apostle or associated closely with an Apostle?' Second, 'Were the contents apostolic in their doctrine and teaching?' Third, 'Was the document used and read by christians as a help in their everyday living?' Early church leaders such as Polycarp, Justin Martyr, Tertullian, Origen, Eusebius, Athanasius, Jerome and Augustine added their approval but did not force their choice on the young church. The final canon emerged through the combined conviction of the early leaders that the twenty-seven New Testament books were 'God-breathed'. The first complete list of the twenty-seven books was mentioned in the Festal letter of Athanasius, Bishop of Alexandria, when he announced the date of Easter in AD 367. The list was then confirmed at the Synod of Hippo in AD 393.

Are The New Testament Sources Reliable?

The earliest New Testament manuscript we have is in the John Rylands Library in Manchester and is a very small piece of John's gospel, dated AD 100–150. There are over 5,000 whole or fragmentary Greek manuscripts in various parts of the world. F. F. Bruce says, 'There is no body of ancient literature in the world which enjoys such a wealth of good textual attestation as the New Testament.'[2]

Dead Sea Scrolls

In 1947 a shepherd grazing his flock in a wadi at Qumran near the Dead Sea, discovered a cave full of jars containing early manuscripts. The most distinguished scholars called the find 'phenomenal' and 'sensational'.[3] The documents, dated between 130 BC – AD 70, were fragments of a library which had belonged to a Jewish monastic community. A complete copy of Isaiah was found in Hebrew which was much older than any other known manuscript. In all, 40,000 fragments were discovered and these have been reconstructed into over 500 books. About 100 of these are copies, with duplicates, of Old Testament books. In a general sense these underline and emphasise the accuracy of the documents we already have.

Which Translation Should I Use?

There are over 350 translations available in English and these fall into three major groups. First, there are *literal translations* which aim to put the words of the original writer into English. The *Revised Standard Version* is a good example of this. In the second group the translators have aimed at what the experts call *dynamic equivalence*. They want their translation to make the same impact on modern readers as the original made on the first readers. A striking example of this is the *Good News For Modern Man* where 'standard, everyday, natural English' has been used. A translation which bridges these two groups, and which is very popular today, is the *New International Version*. The third group consists of paraphrase, and the best example of this is the *Living Bible* which makes the Scriptures eminently readable and understandable. We must use a Bible which is easy to read. For deep study it is essential that we use the best translation available.

1. J. R. W. Stott *Understanding the Bible*, Scripture Union, 1972, p. 227
2. F. F. Bruce *The Book and the Parchments*, Pickering & Inglis, 1950, p. 178
3. *Ibid*, p. 114

8

CONTRADICTIONS AND DIFFICULTIES

In a short volume it would be impossible to refer to all the problems that can be found in the Bible. We will confine ourselves to the Gospels because they are the heart of the christian faith and they are also a happy hunting ground for those who look for contradictions and difficulties. There are three main reasons for the differences in the Gospels.

Aramaic And Greek

First, there is the *difficulty of translation*. Every event and each conversation recorded in the Gospels originally took place in *Aramaic* which was the local language and the common form of Hebrew spoken in that part of the world. A few Aramaic expressions have even been preserved for us by the translators: *Talitha Koum* (Mark 5:41); *Ephphatha* (Mark 7:34); *Abba* (Mark 14:36) and *Eloi Eloi Lama Sabachthani* (Mark 15:34).

However, although Aramaic was spoken by Jesus and the early disciples, it is not the language of the New Testament. Palestine had become part of the Roman Empire in 63 BC and Greek was the common language of the eastern part of the Mediterranean. The Roman Empire was thoroughly bilingual.[1] In Rome you would hear Greek spoken as much as Latin at all levels of society.

The New Testament was written at the time when the Church was expanding into the Roman world and it was therefore quite natural that Greek should be chosen as the language of the New Testament. It was one of the languages used by everybody. However, there was no 'authorised version' of the original Aramaic events and no 'authorised version' of the Greek text. The translators had to work as well as they could. Matthew's 'If a blind man leads a blind man, both will fall into a pit' (Matthew 15:14), becomes Luke's 'Can a blind man lead a blind man? Will they not both fall into a pit?' (Luke 6:39). According to Luke, Jesus said, 'Give what is inside the dish to the poor, and everything will be clean for you' (Luke 11:41). A single-letter change in an Aramaic word would produce 'clean what is in the heart then all is pure' which is not only much more understandable, it also agrees with Matthew (Matthew 23:26). The unfamiliarity of Aramaic can account for some of the differences in the Gospels.

One Wrong Digit

The United States Army Supplies Department has just mistakenly delivered a seven ton ship's anchor valued at $28,560 to an army unit based over 1,000 miles from the sea. The clerk at Fort Carson in Colorado intended to order a new head lamp for a car but typed 4772 into the computer instead of 4972. One wrong digit completely changed the order. In the same way, one wrong letter in translating can produce considerable differences of meaning.

The Dramatic Teaching Of Jesus

Secondly, *the teaching style of Jesus was both imaginative and dramatic*. Everything that Jesus said must be taken seriously, but not always literally. Did He actually see 'Satan fall like lightning from Heaven' (Luke 10:18), or is the graphic expression, 'flash of lightning' simply proof that Jesus was there when it happened and that this dramatic event was indelibly imprinted in His memory? The vivid statement about a soul being eternally punished by its own rotting flesh is a word picture based on Jerusalem's refuse tip in the Hinnom Valley and is borrowed from Isaiah 66:24. The rubbish dump not only included household waste but also

the offal from the animals sacrificed in the Temple. The
Hinnom Valley was a place which bred maggots and the heat
generated by decomposition caused the rubbish to smoulder
continually. If we are to take Jesus literally we must face the
question, 'How can anything that is being destroyed also be
eternal?'

In nearly 2,000 years of christian history there have been
many men of faith who have made many 'iron doors yield',
but not one mountain has been geographically displaced
(Matthew 21:21). As far as I know no planks have actually
been removed from the eye of a beholder enabling 'a speck of
sawdust' to be seen more clearly in a neighbour's eye
(Matthew 7:3). Jesus enshrines truth in vivid metaphor,
image, picture and simile. G. K. Chesterton said 'Jesus had a
vivid literary style of his own.'[2] Misunderstanding must
result if we take Jesus literally when He intended otherwise.
We fall into the trap of Origen who emasculated himself to
cure his lust. That was not what Jesus had in mind. Jesus had
a poet's facility with words and an artist's ability to capture
truth in a few vivid brush-strokes.

Thirdly, behind the Gospels is *the basic source material* of the
life and teaching of Jesus Christ. This *nub* or *kernel* of Gospel
teaching was largely contained in the personal reminiscences
of one or two early disciples. It was treasured, gossiped,
preached, arranged and re-arranged a thousand times before
it came to be written down. When it was recorded this *core*
material was used by the different writers to emphasise the
particular point they were making.

If you compare Matthew's account of the Sermon on the
Mount with Luke's, it's clear that Matthew includes sayings
of Jesus that Luke would suggest were spoken on other
occasions. Luke tells us that the Lord's Prayer was given by
Jesus in direct response to an appeal made by the disciples
when they had seen Him at prayer. While for Matthew it was
part of the Sermon on the Mount. This difference between
the two Gospels doesn't actually mean that either Matthew
or Luke were wrong or that one of them had mis-
remembered the original events. Jesus surely used the same

material on more than one occasion; indeed it is obvious that He did.

What is clear is that the Gospel writers drew from a common source of material. All but thirty-one verses of Mark's Gospel are reproduced in Matthew and Luke, and most of Matthew's remaining material is so similar that it suggests another common source. It is the similarity of the Gospels which is so remarkable, and not their difference.

If you are aware of the difficulty of translating into English an Aramaic text which comes to us through Greek; if you allow for the dramatic language of Jesus; if you make allowances for the individuality of each writer, noting that Luke can be painstakingly literal while Matthew is inclined to spiritualise (see the Beatitudes in Matthew 5:3 and Luke 6:20), then you are well on the way to ironing out the differences in the Gospels. Let me emphasise again that it is the agreement we find in the Gospels which is striking and not the differences.

1. F. F. Bruce *The Books and the Parchments*, Pickering & Inglis, 1950, p. 62
2. G. K. Chesterton *Orthodoxy*, Sheed & Ward, 1939, p. 271

9

THE BIBLE AND SCIENCE

The Bible is not a scientific book; the laws of science are not its main concern. We wouldn't expect an artist painting a sunset to include details of thermodynamics, nor would we expect Shakespeare to give exact sociological themes and perspectives in *The Merchant of Venice*.

The Bible Is Not Unscientific

However, it would be wrong to suggest that the Bible is unscientific. Francis Schaeffer, a major twentieth century writer and thinker, said the Bible

> ... *is* a scientific textbook in the sense that where it touches the cosmos it is true, propositionally true. When we get to heaven, what we learn further will no more contradict the facts the Bible now gives us than the New Testament contradicts the Old. The Bible is *not* a scientific textbook, if by that one means that its purpose is to give us exhaustive truth or that scientific truth is its central theme and purpose.[1]

The purpose of the Bible is to speak to us about God. It shows a God who was there when the world began and who will be there when it ends. The Bible touches on world history so far as man is concerned. We see the broad sweep of history from man's beginning to the time when his redemption was won on the cross. The Bible talks about God's love for man and His desire to see him redeemed. The heart of its message is the life of Jesus and how 'He himself bore our sins in His body on the tree' (1 Peter 2:24).

The Fantasy Of Our Age

Malcolm Muggeridge has said recently that he supposes 'Every age has its own particular fantasies.' He continues, '*Ours is science.* A seventeenth century man like Pascal, who, though himself a mathematician and a scientist of genius, found it quite ridiculous that anyone should suppose that rational process could lead to any ultimate conclusions about life, but easily accepted the authority of the Scriptures. With us it is the other way round.'[2] That exactly sums up the twentieth century. The fantasy of our age is the belief that man can define and answer his own questions without either recourse to God or reference to His Word.

Fortunately there are many twentieth century men of scientific genius who, without compromising their scientific disciplines, are also christian men and are committed to God's word.

A Well Balanced Planet

When you think of the unscientific background of the Old Testament writers, it can be surprising to see how close they are to contemporary scientific thinking. Today, geologists talk of the fine balancing of the earth as it orbits through space. They see the land mass balancing the water mass, keeping the earth stable in its orbit.[3] Isaiah would appear to touch on this when he speaks of a God who 'Measured the waters in the hollow of His hand' and 'Weighed the mountains on the scales and the hills in a balance' (Isaiah 40:12).

The Mysterious Cycle Of Water

The recent droughts in Africa have made us more conscious of the seemingly endless supply of water enjoyed by most people in the northern hemisphere. We see the hydrological cycle of water evaporating from the oceans into the atmos-

phere to form clouds. Then it is redeposited on the earth as
rain or snow. This runs into the streams and rivers and
eventually back into the sea in order that the cycle might
begin all over again. Scientists tell us that before the seventeenth century men were puzzled by this supply of water and
even assumed that there were large subterranean reservoirs
deep in the earth.[4] Yet Job, the author of the oldest book in
the Bible, speaks as clearly as a modern textbook about
evaporation and precipitation: 'He draws up the drops of
water, which distil as rain to the streams; the clouds pour
down their moisture and abundant showers fall on mankind'
(Job 36:27,28). Indeed he appears to understand condensa-
tion: 'He wraps up the waters in His clouds, yet the clouds do
not burst under their weight' (Job 26:8).

Not A Flat-Earth Document

Nicholas Copernicus (1473–1543) seems to have taken most
people by surprise in the sixteenth century with his theory
that the earth was in motion. Then men like Tycho Brahe
(1546–1601), Johann Kepler (1571–1630) and Galileo
(1564–1642) gave birth to modern astronomy with the no-
tion of a universe of quite staggering proportions filled with
an infinite number of planets. Again, much earlier, Isaiah
had spoken of the heavens being 'higher than the earth'
(Isaiah 55:9) and Job suggests the infinity of space as he
exclaims, 'See how lofty are the highest stars' (Job 22:12).
This is underlined by Jeremiah with his suggestion that the
heavens above cannot be measured (Jeremiah 31:37).

The Mystery Of The Universe

The more we learn, the more there appears still to be learnt.
Many years ago I met a scientist who told me that when he
was a student he would light a match and describe exactly
what took place. Scientifically, he would define the wood of
the matchstick, the chemicals that gave ignition, the process
of combustion and the dynamics of the flame. However, he
admitted that as he grew older he couldn't be so exact and

was moved to much greater caution. This was because of the deep mysteries that still surround wood, combustion and flames. Science resolves many problems each year but these solutions only seem to add to the great mystery of the universe.

A Noble Volume

If you want to fly, you will need to understand aerodynamics. If space travel is your forte, then you will need to study astrophysics. If you desire to know God and to understand the way of salvation, the Bible is the volume to which you must turn. Indeed many scientists would regard it as a noble volume which stands quite apart from any scientific journal in the sheer breadth of its teaching. The days have long since past when the scientists thought science would answer all the problems of the universe. In 1865 the Congress of Liege declared, 'Science has made God unnecessary.' It is not as easy as that; deep mysteries still surround the universe. However, the Bible makes truth quite plain.

1. Francis A. Schaeffer *Genesis in Space and Time*, Hodder & Stoughton, 1972, p. 36
2. Malcolm Muggeridge *Jesus Rediscovered*, Collins, 1973, p. 47
3. John F. MacArthur jnr. *Take God's Word For It*, Regal Books, 1980, p. 19
4. John F. MacArthur jnr. *Why I Trust the Bible*, Victor Books, 1983, p. 95

10

JESUS AND THE OLD TESTAMENT

There can be no disputing the fact that both Jesus and his disciples, the founders of Christianity, held and taught that the Hebrew Scriptures, which consist of the Old Testament, were God's Word. Even as late as his letter to Timothy (AD 60–61), we see Paul affirming that all the Hebrew Scripture is 'God-breathed and is useful for teaching, rebuking, correcting and training in righteousness' (2 Timothy 3:16).

The Mischievous Piece Of Paper

Some time ago J. A. Motyer wrote an article entitled *The Mischievous Piece of Paper*. He was referring to the *blank page* that publishers are accustomed to put in between the Old and the New Testaments. This is not part of the Bible and shouldn't be there. Its presence only helps perpetuate the idea of two separate literary *units* when the whole Bible is endeavouring to emphasise the unity of the divine narrative.

The word *Testament* is badly chosen too. The biblical word is *Covenant* (Jeremiah 31:31). It is true to say that the whole Bible is concerned with the *Covenant* God has made with His people and which is first referred to in the divine story as early as Genesis (Genesis 3:15). The words *New Covenant* are themselves Old Testament words (Jeremiah 31:31). Isaiah speaks of the *peace* that the New Covenant will bring (Isaiah 54:10); Jeremiah tells how it will *deal with sin* (Jeremiah 31:34) and Ezekiel informs us that *new birth* will be associated with it (Ezekiel 36:26). In any serious study of the Bible it is much better to disregard the division between the Old and

New Testaments and to see Genesis as the first book in the Bible and Revelation as the last.

Understanding The Old Testament

The turning point of history for the christian is the birth of Jesus Christ. All that happened before that time is labelled BC (Before Christ) and all that follows is AD (Anno Domini). If there is any justification at all in the two literary units it is that the Old Testament is BC and that the New Testament is AD. However, the thirty-nine books of the Old Testament are not in date order; that is, their order is governed neither by their date of writing nor by the timing of the events they speak about. They are grouped into three literary categories *history, poetry* and *prophecy*.

The first five books of the Bible, often called the *Pentateuch*, together with the twelve books that follow, are the *historical* books. They begin with the creation story and the birth of God's people, then follow their history through the captivity in Babylon until the rebirth of the nation under Ezra and Nehemiah.

The *poetry* books, or *wisdom literature*, are the five books which begin with Job and end with the Song of Solomon, including Psalms, Proverbs and Ecclesiastes.

The final division of the Old Testament contains the *prophetical* books and consists of the four *major* prophets (Isaiah, Jeremiah, Ezekiel and Daniel) together with Lamentations and then the twelve *minor* prophets. Augustine tells us that the words 'major' and 'minor' refer to *size* and not importance.

The Hebrew Bible

Some people find it confusing that the christian Bible is not in the same order as the Hebrew Scriptures. The order used in the Bible is the one established by the Alexandrian Jews who translated the Hebrew into Greek in the second and third centuries BC.

The Theme Of The Old Testament

The Old Testament follows a single storyline. It is what the theologians call *Heilsgeschichte*, which is the story of salvation as we see God redeeming His people. This is the reason why so much of the history of the rest of the world is missing from the Old Testament. For example, you won't find any reference to the great Chinese civilisation in the East or very much about the mighty empires that surrounded the Bible lands.

Prophecy

In the Old Testament a prophet is a man who proclaims the Word of God. One main Hebrew word for prophet is *Nabi* and it means *gusher*. Just as an oil well gushes out oil, so the prophet pours forth God's Word. The prophet stands before men and speaks for God (Exodus 7:1). He is God's spokesman.

History Before It Happens

Another aspect of the work of the prophet was *foretelling*. Events are declared and defined long before they happen. At a carol service you will be made aware that long before Jesus was born the prophets announced His birth and said exactly where it would be. But there are prophecies about many other subjects too. In the prophetical books there are at least twenty consecutive chapters in Isaiah where the prophet is foretelling future events which are about to happen; there are seventeen in Jeremiah and nine in Ezekiel.

Let us consider one tiny part of one prophecy which concerns the city of Tyre on the edge of the Mediterranean Sea:

> therefore this is what the Sovereign Lord says: I am against you, O Tyre, and I will bring many nations against you, like the sea casting up its waves. They will destroy the walls of Tyre and pull down her towers: I will scrape away

her rubble and make her a bare rock. Out in the sea she will become a place to spread fish nets, for I have spoken, declares the Sovereign Lord. She will become plunder for the nations (Ezekiel 26:3–5).

Tyre was a Phoenician city and the Phoenicians were a great maritime nation in Old Testament times. They had circumnavigated Africa and established trade routes to the Far East. They had built themselves a magnificent fortified city on the edge of the Mediterranean called Tyre which had very high walls that protected the city on the landward side while the navy protected the sea-approaches.

Three years after Ezekiel's prophecy, Nebuchadnezzar besieged the city. When he finally broke through the walls he found that the inhabitants had taken everything of value to a tiny island half a mile offshore. In his rage Nebuchadnezzar smashed the walls and the towers of Tyre to the ground before going home.

The new community flourished on the tiny island for the next two hundred and fifty years. The prophecy of Ezekiel had been partially fulfilled.

The next conqueror on the scene was Alexander the Great. He had defeated the Persians and then turned to defeat the rest of the world. He arrived in Phoenicia with an army of thirty-three thousand foot soldiers and fifteen thousand mounted cavalry. Alexander called for Tyre's surrender. The Phoenicians felt safe on their island which they had reinforced by building substantial walls once again. Alexander realised that the only way to approach Tyre would be to extend the land in the form of a peninsula out to the island. This he proceeded to do. Nebuchadnezzar's destruction of the towers and walls provided the material and his massive army gave him the workforce. Every scrap of loose rubble and earth was used, indeed Alexander's men had to scrape down to the bed-rock beneath the old city. Huge towers were erected on wheels and rolled across the new causeway enabling the soldiers to climb the walls of the island city. Alexander had also gathered a fleet of ships from the nations he had conquered. He used these to protect the vulnerable peninsular causeway and then to help sack the island.

The prophecy of Ezekiel was now fulfilled much more completely. *Firstly* Nebuchadnezzar had destroyed the towers and the walls. *Secondly*, the hill had been scraped bare to the rock to provide the infilling for the causeway. *Thirdly*, the place where the old city was originally, had now quite literally become the place where fishermen spread their nets. *Fourthly*, Tyre was plundered by the ships of many nations. Ezekiel's prophecy was certainly history written long before it happened.

The Attitude Of Jesus To The Old Testament

They 'testify about me' was one way Jesus spoke of the Scriptures (John 5:39) and they 'cannot be broken' was another (John 10:35). 'I tell you the truth, until heaven and earth disappear, not the smallest letter, not the least stroke of a pen, will by any means disappear from the Law until everything is accomplished' (Matthew 5:18). Throughout His life Jesus reverently submitted Himself to the demands of the Old Testament Scriptures. He firmly emphasised the fact that they spoke about Him. He expected others to believe them and to live by their teaching. There is never any suggestion that He contradicted their teaching or doubted their divine origin.

How Must We Respond?

It is not enough to *possess a Bible* or simply *to read it*, because the Bible wasn't 'designed to be read as literature.' Nor must we regard it superstitiously because in itself it does '*not give life*' but rather *leads 'to the Lifegiver*'.[1] Our aim should not be unapplied 'diligent study' (John 5:39), because that will only produce head knowledge. Jesus obeyed the Scriptures and that must be our response too. John Stott expresses our responsibility so clearly when he says, 'the best way to honour this book as God's book is to do what it says.'[2]

1. Marcus Dodds *The Gospel of John*, Expositors Greek New Testament, Hodder & Stoughton, 1897, p. 745
2. J. R. W. Stott *Christ the Controversialist*, Tyndale Press 1970, p. 104

11

HOW TO USE THE BIBLE

We have looked at how the Bible came into being and how to interpret it. Now, as we come to this final chapter, we need to think about how we get the most out of our Bible as we read it.

The Butterflies, The Bees And The Botanist

There used to be a magnificent garden. The owners occasionally opened it to the public so they too could enjoy its rare species. One day the owner was surveying the beauty of his garden from a sitting-room window when he saw a butterfly fluttering from flower to flower, pausing only for a few seconds on each bloom. It touched many flowers but derived benefit from none. Next, he spotted a botanist with a large notebook under his arm and an enormous magnifying glass in his hand. He spent a considerable amount of time hunched over each bud inspecting it thoroughly through his powerful glass and furiously scribbling notes. Finally, he closed his notebook, put his magnifying glass into his pocket and hurried away.

The third visitor to the flower garden was a tiny bee. The bee would alight on a flower, crawl down deeply into each bloom and fly away with as much nectar as it could carry. On each visit the bee arrived empty and went away full.[1]

We must make certain that when we come to study our Bibles we are not like the *butterfly*, fluttering here and there through the pages and gaining nothing at all. Equally we must not be like the *botanist* who only had an academic interest in his subject. We must imitate the *bee* and delve so deeply into our subject that, as William Tyndale put it, '*we suck out the pith*'[2] of each syllable of biblical truth. Cranmer's prayer about the Scriptures was that we should 'read, mark and inwardly digest them'. Certainly, if we are involved in any kind of specific christian work such as Sunday School teaching or speaking and preaching, and even if we are not, we must 'daily read and weigh the Scriptures' that we might 'wax ripe and strong'[3] to use the delightful language of the Prayer Book.

There used to be a poor Jamaican farmer called Alfred D'Costa who found that nothing would grow on his land, whereas the rest of the island appeared to be extremely fertile, producing coffee, bananas and citrus fruit in abundance. Alfred D'Costa's farm yielded no more than a weedy scrub that hardly covered the soil. In one last attempt to rescue something from his farm in 1942, he sent a sample of the soil for analysis and found that it contained an extremely high proportion of bauxite. Immediately a plant was set up to separate the bright red soil from the finely powdered aluminium oxide which, when smelted, becomes aluminium. Very quickly Alfred D'Costa became an extremely rich man, as the export of bauxite became Jamaica's biggest foreign currency earner and he was honoured by the Queen with a knighthood.

Many people find their Bibles as arid as D'Costa's land. For them it is a wilderness, made even more depressing by the abundant spiritual fruit that others appear to gather. The Bible is like Alfred D'Costa's farm in another way; its treasure has to be patiently mined. There is no easy way to acquire Bible knowledge. Yet once gained, it becomes a vast treasury of truth which can guide our living and thinking in the days to come.

How Not To Use The Bible!

Before Edgar Wallace, a thriller writer of the 1930s, became famous, he was advised by a friend that he should 'turn the key' in his Bible for help.[4] He was told that he should let his Bible fall open at random and point to a verse, expecting God to guide him through what was written. This method is not one to be recommended, in spite of the fact that John Wesley used it; his name for it was 'consulting the oracle'.[5] J. I. Packer tells of a friend who had accepted an invitation to be the minister of a church in the north of England only to be offered a more attractive appointment in the south a few days later. He felt that he couldn't withdraw from the original commitment until his daily Bible reading was 'I say to the North, give up' (Isaiah 43:6 AV). Dr Packer says that this method of Bible study and guidance savours 'more of magic or witchcraft than true' christianity.[6] I would have thought its dangers are more than obvious.

Let Me Be Very Practical

Let me be very practical and deal with the basic essentials for personal Bible study. *Firstly*, we must allow time each day; twenty to thirty minutes as a minimum. *Secondly*, an easy to read translation, such as the *Good News Bible* or the *Living Bible* is helpful for daily devotional study. However, for deeper study, the *Revised Standard Version* would be better or perhaps the *New International Version*, which is probably most frequently used today. *Thirdly*, we must pray for understanding and insight. *Fourthly*, unless we are very disciplined, a system of Bible reading notes such as those produced by the Scripture Union, will be helpful. *Fifthly*, we will need a notebook to use alongside the Bible in order to remember all that we learn. *Sixthly*, we must conclude with prayer and see that the lessons learnt are transferred into daily living.

The Spermatic Word

Justin Martyr called the Bible God's '*Spermatic Word*' and without hesitation I would say that it is the most life-changing piece of literature in the world today. Many people laughed at Adolph Schicklgrüber when he published his thoughts in 1924 entitled *My struggle*. He changed his name to

Adolph Hitler and by the 1940s his thoughts weren't so amusing. For each word of *Mein Kampf* 125 people died in World War II. Those are quite staggering statistics and yet they pale into insignificance when compared with the millions who have found life for each word in the Bible. The life-giving effect of the Bible is nowhere better illustrated than in the history of the christian church in Korea. The Koreans are a people with a very long history and who have developed a culture of their own. Perhaps it was to preserve this culture that they became a hermit people in the last century, closing their country to all foreigners. Yet when the first missionaries arrived in 1884 they found a handful of christians.

Twenty years earlier, God called the Reverend Robert Jermaine Thomas to be a missionary in China. He sailed there in the early 1760s with his wife and a good supply of Bibles. Almost immediately after he arrived his wife died in the most tragic circumstances. Some sort of holiday seemed right for Mr Thomas so, taking his supply of Bibles with him, he travelled to Korea on an American schooner called *The General Sherman*. As the schooner sailed up the Daidong River towards Pyongyang, the northern capital, it was caught on the mudflats. The Koreans, hostile to strangers, executed the passengers and the crew and then set fire to the schooner, having first taken the cargo of Bibles ashore.

Korean houses, like most oriental homes, have little furniture: but they do have highly decorated walls. The India paper of the Bibles seemed just right for wall decoration. No doubt it was the scholars who knew Chinese who appreciated it most and soon a handful of people were not only convinced but also converted to christianity by reading that wallpaper. So when the first missionaries arrived in 1774, they found a church had come into being through the power of the Word of God to bring life. God's Word is *spermatic*; it is life-giving indeed.

He Gives His Word

Do you know the book called Roget's Thesaurus? It is by the English scholar, Peter Roget and is his '*Treasury of English Words and Phrases*'. It is easy to understand why he called it a thesaurus because that is the Greek word for *treasure*. James tells the rich people of his day that they had selfishly 'laid up treasure (thesaurizō) for the last days', but it wouldn't help them (James 5:3 R.S.V.).

The greatest treasury of words is not Peter Roget's but God's and we have that in our Bibles. It is treasure to help us in these last days. So let's excavate the treasure and become rich in God's word. We can do this because *He Gives His Word*.

1. J. F. MacArthur jnr. *Take God's Word For It*, Regal Books, 1980, p. 128
2. William Tyndale *The Five Books of Moses*, 1529, Preface
3. J. I. Packer *Under God's Word*, Lakeland, 1980, p. 186
4. Margaret Lane *Edgar Wallace, Biography of a Phenomenon*, 1938, p. 175.
5. Arnold Dallimore *George Whitefield*, Banner of Truth, 1970, Vol. 1,
6. J. I. Packer *Under God's Word*, Lakeland, 1980, p. 22